T0245772

you

CHANTAL NEVEU

translated by Erín Moure

Literature in Translation Series
Book*hug Press
Toronto, 2024

FIRST ENGLISH EDITION

Published originally under the title *you* © 2021 by Chantal Neveu and La Peuplade. This edition is published by arrangement with Éditions La Peuplade in conjunction with its duly appointed agent BAM, Paris, France.

English translation © 2024 by Erín Moure

ALL RIGHTS RESERVED

No part of this publication may be reproduced or transmitted in any form or by any means, electronic or mechanical, including photocopying, recording, or any information storage or retrieval system, without permission in writing from the publisher.

Library and Archives Canada Cataloguing in Publication

Title: You / Chantal Neveu ; translated by Erín Moure.
Other titles: You. English
Names: Neveu, Chantal, 1964- author. | Moure, Erín, 1955- translator.
Description: A poem. | Translation of: You.
Identifiers: Canadiana (print) 2023048087X | Canadiana (ebook) 2023048090X
  ISBN 9781771668828 (softcover)
  ISBN 9781771668842 (PDF)
  ISBN 9781771668835 (EPUB)
Classification: LCC PS8577.E7597 Y5813 2024 | DDC C841/.54—dc23

The production of this book was made possible through the generous assistance of the Canada Council for the Arts and the Ontario Arts Council. Book*hug Press also acknowledges the support of the Government of Canada through the Canada Book Fund and the Government of Ontario through the Ontario Book Publishing Tax Credit and the Ontario Book Fund.

Cover image: Raw diamond in kimberlite (polyhedral in the rough)

Book*hug Press acknowledges that the land on which it operates is the traditional territory of many nations, including the Mississaugas of the Credit, the Anishnabeg, the Chippewa, the Haudenosaunee, and the Wendat peoples. We also recognize the enduring presence of many diverse First Nations, Inuit, and Métis peoples and are grateful for the opportunity to meet and work on this territory.

you

first his breathing then his pupils

I watch his mouth

its furrows its swells

slight circle of his irises

from the dark hole a tube

he sees me

impulsion

an implicit programmatics

ascension

les façades le quartier

remanence of Rio

a yard a garden

the staircase

winding

its gradations

compelling

the maples

alongside

the black locusts

figuration of caresses

swirled rumour of a fountain

faint sound

metallic taste of the city

a magnetism

from palate to nostrils

infra-resonance

warm silver

low table

the flakes of fish

air under the studio ceiling

a loge

we make acquaintance

summer solstice alters the sky

we deflect curiosity by foreseeing questions

private

spheres

spontaneous revelation

the ineffable

freshness of a stream

are we already naked

bared

we expose ourselves

fluidity

gravity

propensity

the charm

the intimacy

premise of a banquet

Hephaistos

Aristophanes

vestiges Dionysiae vertigos

Empedocles

happiness

tenor of futures put to the test

at ease

we name

great loves

inflections

decades

les fidélités

promises made

offences injuries miracles

the enduring friendships

gaie santé

current genealogy

virtual group portrait

numerous

already

he stands up

draughts

the bamboo imbibe their fill of rainwater

transfer of delectation

euphoria

temptation reparation

congruency

catalysis

paradoxical privilege

incursion

permissiveness

we draw close

we kiss

convergence

watch bracelet undone

dressing table

time an invention

pulsebeats

the curve of the eyelids

we embrace

before

mirror

on my neck

a breath

you are my fantasy

mercurial drape of the curtains

prisms and photons

on the wall

gold

solid

gleaming

velvet at my feet

we revolutionize

the air

between

the legs

we move

are we sleeping

introspective meditation at night

dawn will demand more of us

a disclosure a declaration

I came to make love

fabulous dissolution of a troubling sobriety

mysteries

miseries

topology of fluids

continuum of confidences

an irreducible love

his wife

recognized value of cumulative years

hard work of facing challenges

a visceral hold

an apprehensiveness

devotion

she wants to die in my arms

contiguity

vis-à-vis

my own sediments

alluvium

a recent reversal in love

separation's zigzag

slow wane of triangulations

mapping out a transition

plateau

observatory

reconstruction

new perimeter

morning drawn out

penetrated

in the folds

a light

vertical

splits the bed

marvel

a girl child

awaited met received recognized

adopted

adored

divinity

lineage

marked

on lower back

blue blemish

locus of sensuality

ebb of our sexuality

volcanoes

lake encircled

latency

aftershocks

almas gemelas

they're both coming to join me

we'll sort it out

I'll not be able to touch you

I absorb

le réel

gone pale

she'd catch wind of it

she's very strong

my heart skips a beat

the nerve

shudders

our hands

joined

a line glows

the ring

it's a lot to take in

I go back over it

no room to manoeuvre

I'll be frank with you

as we go along

must keep my wits steady

the meeting blurs the feeling of division

increases it even more

we don't resist the vectors of enthrallment

whatever may happen

envelopment

echo

suspension

we are fully aware

plunge into the vortex

our days are numbered

displacement

without appeal

pairing up

exotic

optimal

bay surrounded by seven hills

cité

emerald

generic

wandering feasts

porosity

beauty of blind walls

glass rhombohedron

immersion

heterogeneous

gestures made freely

anamorphoses

under a chandelier

three-dimensional charisma

inaugural effusion

the water

laps over the ankles

over the wrists

I wash my feet

a ceremony

fine perspiration

behind the knees

openings

in the dusk light

mauve

the touch of his thumbs

newly prehensile

advent of a consensual dependence

initiatory

gentleness

expression of his virility

head in the corridor

back and kidneys

the floor

its astonishing thinness

we laugh

throats abdomens pressed

we recognize

inner figures

we fathom each other

molecules vibrate

we are proportional

creation of a myth

against the mountain flank

the afternoon

neck bent

bowed

raised again

to hear the cardinal

singing

gorgeous

the female redbird come back

privileging détente

perfecting my polyhedric practices

flowing in his direction

I will empty myself out

nothing visible

reverse osmosis

in the meshes of the city

a life simple and secret

sumptuous resistance to capitalizations

to demoralization

an asceticism

fervour

lying at his feet

head pillowed by books

letting myself doze

he works

alongside

my sleep

a watch over

an improvised desk

ripe fruits

the soil is rare

gone

into the east

5,700 kilometres

unlimited ceiling

we'd not bade each other

farewell

nor goodbye

arrogant confidence of lovers

not doubting time or space

holding a thread

ductile

becoming adept at our conversations

nets of syntax

deductions retorts relays

the familiar the surprising

emotions

heady vocabulary

tessitura

delights

congruence

constitutive matter in deep layers

shared love of intervals

the atmosphere

the architectonic

the crown of trees

the cobalt in green

the astronomic

amnion eros cosmos

you know how to read me

yet I'm wary of the mediatization

of voices

of our bodies

in space is not in situ

how will we deal with touch

thirty or forty millimetres of water

two cloudbursts

discrete storm cells

a phenomenon of exception

she knows you are present in my life

having noted the thermal shift

suspected a liaison

sought proof

uncovered the letters

left inadvertently

in plain sight

negligence

slip-up

laxity

revelation strategy

transparency would have been preferable

facing up to

the complexity of the situation

entering

deliberately

into the chaos

physically

while trying to minimize suffering

the havoc

more pernicious

cruel

you precede me

manoeuvring in the undecidable

the absence

expectations alter spontaneity

receiving only cellular undulations

no proposition without severe restrictions

outside

elsewhere

a missed call

sudden sense of deficit

voice deferred

increasingly wrenching

communicating vessels

exploring amorous alienation

from another angle

see-saw back again

rigour once imposed on a lover

alignment of expectations

tacit

explicit

with a man

my husband

aerobatics slate turbulences arcana

sophistication

sentimental valences

enigma of attunements

Dos Aguas

the irreproducible

anchorage

extreme

gratitude

waiting before bringing the bamboo inside

it's not perturbed by early cold

innocent of what's meant by subtractive machine

winged seeds dangle from branches

making tea

nothing is

and the air

the image

his sustenance

in passing

the names of streets

of buildings

bridges stations

delta dam

the shimmer of the sky

filtration garden

terraces

Pearl River

Three Gorges

mouth of the Tigris

Doppler effect

bursts

laughter

impetuous wakings of the child

perspicacity of her questions

a lovely husky voice

traduction

malfunction breach

concentration

oracle

what he wants

what he forgets

the dimple of your navel

landscapes

Delphic

domestic

superimposed

he loses his glasses

imagining his eyes encircled by tortoise-

shell

dark-speckled

an aestheticizing compensation

lack of presence

minor jealousies

mother-of-pearl jewellery

on a writing desk

the beam of the lamp

on top of his hand

symptoms of bigger pitfalls

vanity

battling against narcissism

debating myself

surplus of idealization

scoria of idealism

powerlessness

to no longer be

in the same field

optical

haptic

shortcomings magnified

entropy

case study

opportunity for knowledge

expectant psyche

my cascades of tears prophetic

one evening

harsh foreboding

a dubious relationship

difficult candid configuration

meanders

deficiencies

I dedicate my maturity to you

is sublimation the only option

opposite slopes of a summit

tutelary figures

mountain

diamond

pyramid

world magnified

fantasies on a shoreline

high tide

I think of you constantly

irresistible scenarios

extravagant arrangements

feeling caught in a chasm

emerging clairvoyant

in counterpoint

concrete references

the company I keep

corporeal

bookish

friendly

what I bite off

swallow

the syntagmas

the chapters

the appellations

the first fruits

flavours

trajectories

in midtown

to the west

in the North

lakes

Bois-Francs

weather forecast

construction site by a river

concrete slab

poured

polished

rising

cherrywood planks

a staircase

stringers

blurt out

asking him

what do you expect of me

the future

it's spoken

complicit happy serious

affirmative

he regrets

immediately

having clarified that destination

marked out

a Platonist

cavern

the infinitely indefinite

cardia point clenched

a signal

diffuse pain along every meridian

ancestral cartography

needles angled in

anatomic information

voracity of intuitions

nullity of double dyads

impermeability and discretion are not enough

previous admixtures offer me no clues

once again he faces my tears

baroquisme of our eros

in his hand

my voice probing into the labyrinth

the words reach his veins

he walks

fully male

along the quay

I have to interrupt you

have to go

I'm heading inside

later

on a rebound

a fervour

I want you fully

desire to possess you entirely

six time zones rising and falling

how to do it

saturation blocks infiltrations

theatre of the all-powerful

captivity

epistolary life is not life together

sentimentality is not vitality

vice versa

I metabolize

empirical

calibrations

decanted

readings

fabric suppleness density

pattern

floral

geometric

fractal

embroidering

hypnotic

designs in silk

Riemannian patchwork

reiteration

crystallization

an injunction

vivid

dazzling incomprehensible real

constricted

love is discriminator

my body belongs to you

I am chaste

is any existential plane untouched by eros

you ask me to pull myself together

I'm undecided

exiled

we both agree

desire generates aberrations

love is bigger than any of us

a greater destiny

inertia

change of air mass

I keep jettisoning

simulacra

projections

particles of nostalgia

is it possible to forget

the profusion of accompaniments

places ambiences gestures

fabrics

the epidermis

the unprecedented

and our kisses

I let him know

he's still mesmerized

you are summoned in all your splendour

the snares of exaltation detectable

of delectation

enhanced value

the vain promises

the interferences the retractions

he bides his time

just trust me

a clearing

agility

jolt

a boldness

I suggest rupture

explosion

woman of little faith

a sting

raging at the injustice

the righteous tone

hyperbolic

over-rationalizing is unreasonable

easing up

splitting up

celebrating the affinities

our motivations

their difference

admitting the impasse

the nobility of contingencies

the priority

acquiescence

protecting the child

from separation

from abandonment

from parental anguish

spare her the intrusion of a woman

stranger

my person

third wheel

my daughter my legacy

shock wave

we're exhausted

setback reversed

inexplicable

limbic

we resume our concertations

the dismemberment

the inextinguishable

launch back into hypothetical rendezvous

fitting myself into a busy schedule

absorbing

a reality structured

tectonic

impassioned

crisis at its peak

lesson learned late

Montaigne

the benefits of diversion

oxygenation

in the forest

dilatation

reliance

rereading

the Huainanzi   Le Huainan zi

Originating in the Way   Du commencement du réel

Quintessential Spirit   La propension naturelle des êtres

Surveying Obscurities   De l'examen des choses obscures

A Forest of Persuasions   Les tendances affectives

Terrestrial Forms   Des formes terrestres

scripting pointing pushing chuckling condensing

sleeping

reformulating reversing leaping reeling rallying

opening

questioning

Lou Andreas-Salomé

Spinoza Diel Ogien Klein

Graziani Sloterdijk

Roustang Feldenkrais

engramming

poplar catkins in full bloom

perfume of linden

tossing water-gorged cherries into the salad

June

vacation time coming

breaststroke in grottoes

plenitude

aquatic

erotic

canicular

attentive to allusions

noting subtle disinformation

is it intentional

confirming devastation of further delays

the asymmetry

the impact

the hesitations

the irrefutable indications

insight

sagacity

inefficiency

hit by side effects

ambivalence outwits my passivity

noticeable

deceptive resistance

jaw clenched

dark eye circles

and weight loss

another hint

depletion

compensatory words act to dematerialize

I let go

sadness wanes

grief falls away

the obsession

persists the attraction

a question is asked of me

holographic

catalyst or inhibitor

point de retournement

shutting down the radar

swimming

with ions

sepia

keeping to myself to dissolve the ache

fine-tuning the missing liberatory share

lying fallow

you raze your fields

choosing

new speed regime

cruise

I'm in the thick of it

moving forward

writing

four reams

ivory

wisteria coral peony-pink

choral

alto

ictus

silent breath inward

Libera Me

Fauré Andy Moore

Kyriakides

Murcof Martes

Norma

track twelve

Purcell

a relentless bass

eight-beat

hushed voice

I dreaded your dismissal

intolerable fragmentation

in part is not part of

changing operating mode

rebalancing phosphorus levels

the bouquets of daisies

trimming the stems

feeling suddenly placid

of jade

it's all for the best

stay rigorous

stay free

steer the course

stoic

holding to silence

to nothing

you clear space

sense of renunciation

of what never even happened

desolation

the weight of rupture

pride

lassitude

defeat

violence

residue of velleity

safeguard against recidivism

health reflex

ultimatums prohibited

abolition of privations

excess composure gone to dust

withdrawal from potential

recapitulation

it was he who left

imposed a double temperance

conscious unconscious

retention

auction of favours

of retreats

an enclave

fatal non-inclusion

inaccess

we weren't able to create the conditions of presence there
was no external sign or critical sum or tipping point no
decisive action who really knows just a disastrous abso-
lute factitious shifting horizon we satiate ourselves in
other ways let's neutralize the afflictions the arabesques
the neuroses the adversities uncover metaphors lures
plot twists the antagonisms the missteps the obstinacy
the drying up the restagings of family mythology hero-
ism archetypes transgressions overflows psychic or bio-
graphical complacencies historicity the generations ages
classes continents dreams fertile mental soil fundamental

intellect cerebrum cherished carnal organ we like each

other are we losing each other we'll not make love again

my love we live and let live

reorientation

dilution

dislodging myself

staying at the edge of heartache

healing with similars

infinitesimal toxin

tap the bottle

water dynamized

new memory

rejuvenation

elucidation

primacy of his predilection

assertive woman

quintessence

compared to

Venus-like apparition

posture of Olympia

full-on Maja

expressing desires

available

requesting nothing

you dispense with words

you piss before the man you love

integration

inclination

politic

in his eyes

the character of the wife's demands

a pledge

guarantee of mobilization

intrinsic vigour of the union

surface negotiating-game

deep-rooted commitment

leaven of the unbreakable bond

longevity

sibylline pact

abstention

stylistics of the argument

a love pre-eminent

memorial

incontestable matrix

juncture of growth

capital

the library

election

maternal matrimonial

lair

permanence

purpose

speculation

certification

I've gone back home

airlock

rays pivots rivets

extraordinary

the romantic liaisons

effervescences

satellite events

with careful precautions

recentring

a clarity

finally

disengagement

assumption

my heart feels lighter

recoup

transition clemency progression

l'à-venir

honouring the initial induction

the immediate joyous adhesion

vocal

physiological

sensual

the whole sequence

esteem

stimuli

loyalty

the state of being in love

reciprocal

provisional prolonged frustrated

metamorphosed

dual navigation

willingness illusions

balm

voluptuousness momentum work

put to use

aplomb

re-enchantment

unparalleled degree of autonomy

stamina

enriched

high spirits

en silence

an indulgence

flamboyant

a synergy

existential

material

vegetal

circadian

embodied

crepuscular

holistic

diurnal

to better comprehend

the inhibited

the reversible

the sublime

the air

most serene

sovereign

vitality

rib cage

plexus

sacred

solar

hemispheres

decrystallized

moving

out of the thrall

literally

setting out again

from the belvedere

mortal

nonchalant

willingly

plainsong

YOU, VIA ME
(A TRANSLATOR'S POSTFACE)

Chantal Neveu's long poem *you* draws her minimalism to a high and singular pitch, in which the drama of the central voice seems situated then abandoned, amorous then devastated, then free. If *you*'s exploration of a love relation breaks out of a lineage, it might include Jean Cocteau's *La voix humaine* (1928) in French or Elizabeth Smart's *By Grand Central Station I Sat Down and Wept* (1945). In capturing the tenor of the voice in every stage of a love affair, situating "her" in relation with the other, *you* unfolds all the complexity of human relation, of body and health, of *eros* and *logos*, attuned to the larger world of philosophy and literature and elucidating the possibility of habitation, of grandeur, of thinking, of self.

you is one fractal of the exploration of the notion of *idyll* that Neveu gave us in *This Radiant Life*. Composed around the same time (2010–2020), both poems have a similar cadence. Rather than being an exploration of the *gangue*, the source rock for gems and ore (there are references to this space and texture in *TRL*), though, *you* is one of the precious metals, a gem extracted from its rocky source.

you, in exploring idyll, shows us it is not always bucolic joy. Poetically and rhythmically, the text works to articulate the polyhedric nature of human relations: there is never one surface, never two or three, but as many facets as there are in a gemstone. An individual holds not just one position in this relation, this polyhedron, but many, not all at once, and not all contiguous. Sometimes, in reading, we find ourselves facing one way, only to realize we are facing in the opposite direction. The intricacies of human relation displace across bevelled surfaces only to bend light in another direction, across another surface. It is here, in these polyhedric and faceted movements, where we as individuals find our place, create ourselves, free ourselves, begin and begin again. Our singular voice is never *really* singular, but resonates through others, passes through others, rebounds off others, slips and arises from others. Our genders mix up; it is a plurality that gives rise to our *I*, our awareness of self.

How does a human become who she is, who he is, who they are? How do we brave to grasp the presence of the other, allow ourselves to be interpellated, made permeable? Neveu explores the questions, though her words offer no easy answers. In following her, we too live their complications, and emerge—with the poet—able to turn toward new questions.

you does its work on all these pulsions and questions via language itself, not via narrative. It uses a vertical unfolding, in which words and short lines reverberate in a visible field of space. It is we, as readers receiving the text, who construct narrative connections, even when indices are sparse and at times angled away from us. Here we find ourselves in a text that calls to the other, that addresses the self as "you" via the mouth of the other, that addresses "he," that is "he" addressing "she" as the narrator observes, that is "I." The shifts of this intrigue of voicings are received as a whole, for they are not separated for us by typography or expressly identified (and the indices for identification are fewer in English, for we don't have gendered participles and adjectives). The figures merge, turn, emerge.

In the movement of *you*, the vocable "you" is seldom uttered in English (and not at all in the French, which uses "tu," a much more delineated word). This movement contains the reader at the same time as it objectifies "someone"—the poet, the voice that narrates, another person in relation. It is a movement that acts as a counter-valence or counter-rhythm in the text; its pull and push, its revelation of different surfaces, reveal to us an experience of the polyhedric. Here in English now, the textual voice calls upon all the multiplicity of the "you," addresses the self as "you," addresses "he," *is* "he" addressing "you" who is the narrator observing, is "I."

"You" in English can be singular or plural (we've pretty much lost the informal or intimate "thou" and its plural "ye"), and even neutral: we use it to say things like "You must wash your hands" to avoid the passive construction of "Hands must be washed" or the imperative "Wash hands." The "you" softens, includes us; we use it to address ourselves, to describe a state of things or an experience to ourselves, or others. Neveu took this English word as her book title in French, for it is intimate and formal, plural and singular, neutral all at once. She has no need to choose between "tu," "vous," or "on," between the intimate singular, the formal singular, the plural, and the neutral. The word "you" reverberates as foreign in French, which it doesn't do in English, but all the other modalities of the word are with us. It is an accusative, an address, an invitation, an intimacy, and a varying in tonality is part of its constellation: "oh you" can sound sweet and affectionate; "you" on its own is always, as well, the start of something, a sentence, a phrase, an insistence, and an invitation to the other. It is truly a charged particle.

As Neveu has said: "The book *you* engages a relationship to the other (singular, plural, masculine, feminine, and self, etc.), as well as an intrinsic reflection on poetic address itself. My challenge was to further distill this dense material and to find an original form, not apparently narrative, and generous enough to render freely, tonally, and as fluidly as possible the complexity of love and love relationships."*

Neveu insists on the work of words, one word at a time. "Les mots mêmes," a Paul-Marie Lapointe line that was epigraph to *This Radiant Life*, is pertinent here as well.

As a translator, I can't work with a poet's intentions, of course, only with her words. And Neveu's faceting of the single word in French is altered in English: one word in French may be two words or a bundle of words or suffixes in English; the sound values contained in a suite of words may lose their sound relation in the new language, and gain other relations. As I've written in other places,** the act of translating makes me aware of the Glissantian "trembling thinking" that is inherent in my own language, and in language itself. I work

---

*   From an unpublished text dated December 11, 2020, and shared with me by Chantal Neveu.

**   https://hopscotchtranslation.com/2023/01/22/moure-en-passant/

with what I receive as a reader, which comes line by line, condensed, at times one word alone and at times more; I work with the spacing above and below the line, attend to how the line rhythmically spaces and verticalizes the page. Neveu uses the single word as ideogram, almost, in a vertical reading, an enchainment that—except in one place of furious utterance—resists the horizon, that relies on sound and connotational ripples that are spatialized, rather than relying on syntax. Translating just the word, though, would fail, as there's such a shimmer and resonance *between* the lines, particularly in their acute condensations, so that though Neveu might emphasize her scripting as occurring word by word, I translate line by line, conscious of spacings.

Other translators echo my experience. I think of Jennifer Croft, speaking of translating Olga Tokarczuk's *The Books of Jacob* from Polish, saying "sentences" where I would say "line by line": "The words of the text are the embodiment of its past. Its sentences, on the other hand, lead the way into its future, and in so doing, they also pass through the vast, dynamic labyrinth of the translator's imagination."*

In other words, the lines pass through the translator's body, for that is where the imagination is, after all. And translating Neveu *is* a visceral experience. It felt to me that at times I was reading *you* with my veins, with my animality and physicality and not with my frontal cortex, with my brain. It was

* https://lithub.com/the-order-of-things-jennifer-croft-on-translating-olga-tokarczuk/

pulling through me like a cord, as if my veins or nerves were pulled, extended, twisted by the text, and my brain was understanding that twisting and pull. Who was reading who? In *you*, there's a haunting, a spectre, love's spectral move between persons in attraction, inner and outer pulls, histories, loyalties, conversions, metamorphoses, fusions, de-fusions, sovereignties. The dream of love, what is it? Is it just $1 + 1$? Clearly not. Is it 3? Clearly it is much vaster than 3. It is a Riemann sum, converging or diverging. Do we have to give up its dream to truly inhabit our self? Or is the dream of love, in dreaming, transformed and transforming? Does love's dream change us for good, and for the better...?

AUTHOR'S ACKNOWLEDGEMENTS

Happy and grateful for the agreement between Book*hug Press, La Peuplade, and BAM/Books And More Agency, I warmly thank radiant team *you*—dearest Hazel Millar and Jay MillAr, with Stuart Ross, Reid Millar, Charlene Chow, Rachel Gerry, Laurie Siblock, and Michel Vrana: thank you for your trust, your attention, your know-how, elegance, visions, and projections. Thank you for your welcome into the Literature in Translation Series | Poetry which brings *you* to readers in English via the exceptional language-poesia of Erín Moure.

Thank you, Erín, for inviting me into this transformative linguistic experience and allowing me to be a close witness of your translation modus and of your original, rigorous, joyful, lucid, elucidating, integrated way of hearing. With you, the synergy of creation—as much internal and subjective as external and objective—exists in a privileged relationship between sensory and intellectual spheres, emotions, perceptions, and questions. Thank you, amiga poeta Erín Moure, for this enrichment, and thank you for your deep commitment to delivering a splendid writing-translation of *you*, solid in the air, concentrated and reflexive, pluri-dimensional and open—vibrant.

Thank you to *Four Way Review* (USA) which published an excerpt from this work in their Fall 2023 issue.

And, to you, dear readers, who hear and recreate *you*, thank you.

ABOUT THE AUTHOR

LAURENCE GRANDBOIS BERNARD

CHANTAL NEVEU is the author of seven books of poetry: *you*; *La vie radieuse*; *coït*; *mentale* (all La Peuplade); *Une spectaculaire influence* (l'Hexagone); *èdres* (É=É); and *Dans l'architecture* (co-written with Nicolas Tardy, Rhizome). She has also created numerous interdisciplinary literary works, produced and presented in Canada and Europe. Her work has appeared in many magazines and anthologies, including *Cyclages/Grupmuv* (École des arts visuels et médiatiques/ UQAM), *Espaces de savoir* (Université Laval), and *Laboratoire parcellaire* (OBORO/La Peuplade), and she has held residencies at Maison de la poésie de Nantes (France), Passa Porta and Villa Hellebosch (Belgium), and Villa Waldberta (Germany). Book*hug Press has published three previous books by Neveu: *Coït* (tr. Angela Carr); *A Spectacular Influence* (tr. Nathanaël); and *This Radiant Life* (tr. Erín Moure), winner of the 2021 Governor General's Literary Award for Translation and the 2021 Nelson Ball Prize. Chantal Neveu is based in Tiohtià:ke/Montreal.

ABOUT THE TRANSLATOR

E. SAMPEDRIN

ERÍN MOURE is a poet and poetry translator who lives in Tiohtià:ke/Montreal. Her translation of Chantal Neveu's *This Radiant Life* (Book*hug Press, 2020) won the 2021 Governor General's Literary Award for Translation from French and the Nelson Ball Prize. Her most recent poetry translation is Chus Pato's *The Face of the Quartzes* (Veliz Books, 2021) from Galician. Her nineteenth book of poetry, a hybrid work, is *Theophylline: a^n ^{a}po^{r}etic migration via the modernisms of Rukeyser, Bishop, Grimké* (House of Anansi, 2023).

COLOPHON

Manufactured as the first English edition of
you
in the spring of 2024 by Book*hug Press

Copy-edited by Stuart Ross
Proofread by Laurie Siblock
Type + design by Michel Vrana

Printed in Canada

bookhugpress.ca